LIFE SKILLS FOR TEENS

THE BUILDING BLOCKS OF LIFE

How To Execute The Next 10 Years With Finesse

Tara Bass

Table of Contents

Chapter 1: Life Skills For Teens 6
Chapter 2: Beginning In A New Stage of Life 10
Chapter 3: 5 Ways Understanding Psychology For Teens 13
Chapter 4: Don't Make Life Harder Than It Needs To Be 18
Chapter 5: Take Ownership of Yourself 23
Chapter 6: 10 Signs of Teenage Depression 26
Chapter 7: 6 Steps To Get Out of Your Comfort Zone 30
Chapter 8: How To Live Your Best Life 36
Chapter 9: Becoming A Leader 39
Chapter 10: Become A High Performer 42
Chapter 11: Becoming High Achievers 46
Chapter 12: Believe in Yourself 51
Chapter 13: Block Out The Critics and Detractors 53
Chapter 14: Bounce Back From Failure 56
Chapter 15: Building Confidence 59
Chapter 16: Confidence: The Art of Humble-Pride 62
Chapter 17: Change Your Environment For Success 64
Chapter 18: Changing How You Think 67
Chapter 19: Contribute To Society In A Meaningful Way 71
Chapter 20: Dealing with Career Pressure 75
Chapter 21: Dealing With Addictions 78
Chapter 22: Dealing With Addiction To Technology 81
Chapter 23: Dealing With Difficult People 85
Chapter 24: Dealing With Feelings of Failure 89
Chapter 25: 7 Ways To Deal With Personal Selfishness 92
Chapter 26: Dealing With Stress From All the Angles 95
Chapter 27: Discomfort Is Temporary 98
Chapter 28: Develop A Habit of Studying 101

Chapter 29: Doing The Thing You Love Most 104
Chapter 30: Don't Fear Judgement 107
Chapter 31: Don't Live Your Life In Regret 110
Chapter 32: Enjoying The Journey 113

Chapter 1:

Life Skills For Teens

Teenage Life

This is the most delicate phase in a person's life. To most adults who are still 'discovering' themselves, the rain started beating them in their teenage hood. The teen years (thirteen to nineteen) are delicate and need to be paid much attention to before things go haywire.

Importance Of Teenagerhood

This defining time in a person's life is marked by many events. One is neither a child nor an adult and this brings confusion because teenagers require special handling. Parents, guardians, and caregivers contribute a lot to the welfare of their teenagers. Their action or inaction at this stage is not negligible.

Teens are largely neglected because most of them are stubborn with a sense of entitlement. They are not to blame for such behavior (but we can blame growth if we have to). It requires adults to go out of their way and reason with them.

In reasoning with teenagers, there are important life skills that they must be taught for them to grow well.

1. Decision Making

This is a very important skill for everyone but most especially for teenagers. Most people make wrong decisions at this stage and they regret them later in life.

Teens should be taught that it is okay to delay decision-making. It is hardly a matter of life and death. It requires careful considerations of all variables before settling on any choice.

Since most teens decide based on the face value of most things, they should learn that not everything is beneficial although it may appear attractive.

Adults should walk with teenagers in their decision-making journey as closely as possible yet at the same time give them the freedom to choose what they want. It is incumbent upon the adult to advise the young one on what is best. Whether or not they act upon the advice is not the liability of the adult. Choices have consequences.

2. Discipline

Knowing the right thing to do and not thinking twice before doing it is the hallmark of discipline.

Having discipline or the lack of it can be traced back to one's early years. They ignored simple rules at home and extended the same to school. Either out of ignorance or lack of instruction, their indiscipline ways continued even in adulthood.

Most people engage in drugs in their young adult life. It becomes too late to stop when they realize they are on the wrong path. It might presently be uncomfortable for teenagers because of the fear of missing out from what their unruly peers are doing, but they stand to benefit a lot in their future.

3. Networking

Sadly, even some adults do not have this critical life skill. Networking is making friends, in the right way, with people wherever you go. It should be in the right way because befriending truants is not networking.

Networking is with people in different capacities in society for they can be of help in the future. From your teenage life up to young adulthood, you are most likely to meet with destiny connectors. These same people will stand up for you with a positive testimonial that will be of great help in the future.

Teenagers should be courteous towards those they meet because the future is uncertain. They could need the help of the same person they belittled some time back.

4. Tolerance

It is the patience to persevere in short-term unfavorable conditions. Nothing is permanent – even hardships. When you learn patience from an early age, you can be able to wait for your time to shine. Most teenagers want to fulfill their desires there and then. This mad rush for success is the downfall of many people.

Good things surely take time. When a teenager decides to take on a shortcut in life, doom waits for him ahead. These are some life skills that make a difference in the life of a teenager. Pass them down to raise a responsible society.

Chapter 2:

Beginning In A New Stage of Life

A new stage of life can come from an awakening of our self-understanding. We begin to see ourselves differently and clearly. The result is that we may have to make a change in one or more areas of our life.

Another stage is when we experience a significant change in our relationships. Maybe it is marrying for the first time or the birth of your first child. It could even be the change in self-perception that comes following a divorce.

A final example is a stage where we experience a change in jobs or our career direction.

In the first chapter of Circle of Impact: Taking Personal Initiative to Ignite Change, I tell the story of William. He experiences a mid-career transition that requires him to look deeply into his life. He does not have a clear option to remain with the company he served since he graduated from college. He has to decide what this new stage of life will look like.

It is not accidental that new stages of life can be understood from the perspective of the Circle of Impact. For the transition is prompted by one or more of the three dimensions of leadership.

For William, the company (Structure) is changing, and William's family situation (Relationships) requires him to leave the company and begin a new career. William's challenge is understanding what his purpose is, what his skills are, and how both can be marshaled for employment in a new arena.

A new stage of life is less like moving into a new house just like the old house, and more like moving from a cabin in the woods into a high-rise luxury condominium. If we don't treat the change as significant, we find ourselves trying to be a square peg fitting into a round hole.
In effect, we need to step back, pay attention to what is different, listen to what is now expected of us, and allow ourselves the change of mind to fill the role where we will be for the foreseeable future.

Let's take this all too human experience to a deeper level.

You aren't just moving into a new stage of life. This stage requires you to exhibit genuine leadership.

The first step is acknowledging that this new stage will challenge you in new ways.

The next step is to take the three dimensions of leadership and apply them to your new situation. Ask these questions:

1. Are we clear about our purpose? Do we have a clear set of core values that can guide us in our decisions? Are we clear about the expectations for each person's performance?

2. What steps do I need to take to build trust between myself and those whom I'm now leading? Am I clear in my understanding of what each member of the team brings to our work? Do we have the people to cover all aspects of our work together?

3. What kind of structure do we need to maintain a clear focus, good communication, and ensure that we are creating the impact that we desire?

New positions of responsibility require us to also ask these questions.

1. What are my strengths for this new role?

2. What are my limitations? Do we have people on our team whose are strengths are my limitations?

3. Am I prepared to make hard choices? Do I understand what it means for me to operate with integrity?

We all face changes in new stages of life. Some of them project us into areas in which we feel unprepared. If we apply the Circle of Impact model of leadership in each new situation we encounter, we'll find that we come to have a clearer self-understanding and that we are better prepared to make decisions that are necessary.

As you look forward, what do you expect your life to become in the coming years? Anticipating what might come, and actively preparing for that reality will strengthen your self-perception. As a result, a new stage of life that previously would not have been possible now is.

Remember each day to take personal initiative to make a difference that matters, and you'll be prepared for whatever new challenge or opportunity that comes your way.

Chapter 3:

5 Ways Understanding Psychology For Teens

Adolescence is an exciting transition from childhood to adulthood. This year can be filled with exciting discoveries as teens develop their unique personality traits and skills. Some problems accompany the growth process. Adolescents are fundamentally different from children and adults, so it is vital to understand them better to support them as they grow.

Adolescence is a period of significant change for youth, not to mention everyone involved in their lives. During adolescence, it is essential to develop character and independence. At the same time, they grapple with issues such as sex, drug use, and peer relationships, increasing the demand for responsible and reliable people. Adolescent psychology helps you understand your youth and transition from child to adult.

The American Academy of Pediatrics describes adolescence as rapid development in five key areas: moral, social, physical, cognitive, and emotional. To support this development, adolescent psychology focuses on people's mental health issues between the ages of 13 and 19. Adolescent psychologists recognize and support adolescents during this period of growth and transition.

1. Physical/Sexual Development

From the point of view of adolescent psychology, this period of brain development is critical. During this stage, areas of the brain that allow adolescents to control their behaviour and emotions and sites for calculating risks and rewards develop significantly. Teenagers can also think more efficiently due to myelin and brain synapses changes.

All of these physical changes affect the way young people think and act. They can develop sexual awareness and become sexually active. As long as they are healthy, their bodies will be stronger and more harmonious than ever before, making them stand out in sports. Adolescents have many opportunities and challenges when it comes to physical development. The psychology of adolescents can help them understand the material changes they are going through so they can respond positively.

2. Cognitive Development

Along with physical development, adolescence brings new ways of thinking. Adolescence acquires the ability to think abstractly as they develop cognitively. At this stage, imagination and complex reasoning grow exponentially. This gives teens the ability to understand abstract concepts in advanced math and start thinking more about spirituality and love.

When you are a teenager, your thoughts become complicated. They can imagine what their future might be like, but they find it challenging to apply these ideas in their decision-making process. They are also more suspicious of things. In late adolescence, adolescents begin to think differently outside of themselves. They can think more about what is happening globally and society's significant problems. They may also worry about career choices and what to do after leaving home.

3. Emotional Development

Teenagers these days want and need privacy. It's okay. You may be concerned about your appearance and have problems with your body image. By the time you reach your late teens, you will become more confident in yourself and your beliefs. They seek sensory experiences and can be easily sexually aroused. In late adolescence, you begin to control your emotions better. The majority of adolescent psychology is interested in teaching adolescents how to manage their feelings.

4. Moral Development

Teens morality also develops during adolescence. They move in stages of development of power and social order, emphasizing rules. As we get older, we begin to analyze social contracts and relationships. They are committed to doing mutually beneficial and morally right things, even when they are not legally correct. As we age, our moral focus may change again as we begin to think of "right" and "wrong" as universal concepts that apply to different legal systems and cultures.

5. Adolescent Identity

Along with other aspects of cognitive, emotional, and social development, adolescents form their unique personalities at this stage. Their thinking is influenced by adolescent egocentrism but diminishes with age from early to late adolescence. Three characteristics of adolescent egocentrism are:

- Self-immersion: Their focus is almost entirely on themselves.
- Personal Fables: They see themselves as special and unique.
- Imaginary Audience: They think other people pay attention to them and everything about them, including what they say and do.

With all these changes, it is normal for young people to face challenges. Adolescent psychology addresses essential issues that can have a lasting impact on a teenager's life. These include independence, sexual behaviour, drug use, and peer relationships. As adolescents go through these exciting and challenging stages of development, they may need the help of a youth psychologist to address and positively address these issues. Through this experience, they learn to deal with difficult situations and become more independent. Take time each day to strengthen your relationship with your teen. Go for a walk, have a coffee, take them to dinner, or join a class together. They show interest in things they care about (e.g. music, books, activities, sports, friends). This will give you a chance to talk about other things and maintain a healthy relationship with them.

Chapter 4:

Don't Make Life Harder Than It Needs To Be

Today we're going to talk about a topic that I hope will inspire you to make better decisions and to take things more lightly. As we go through this journey of life together, and as we get older, we soon find ourselves with more challenges that we need to face, more problems that we need to solve, and more responsibilities that we need to take on as an adult. In each phase of life, the bar gets set higher for us. When we are young, our troubles mostly revolve around school and education. For most of us we don't have to worry much about making money or trying to provide for a family, although I know that some of you who come from lesser well-off families might have had to start doing a lot earlier. And to you I commend you greatly. For the rest of us we deal with problems with early teenage dating, body image, puberty, grades, and so on. It is only until we graduate from university do we face the harsh reality of the real world. Of being a working adult. It is only then we really forced to grow up. To face nasty colleagues, bosses, customers, you name it. And that is only just the beginning.

Life starts to get more complicated for many of us when we start to realize that we have to manage our own finances now. When our parents stop giving us money and that we only have ourselves to rely on to survive. Suddenly reality hits us like a truck. We realize that making our own money becomes our primary focus and that we may not have much else to rely on. We take on loans, mortgages, credit card debts, and it seems to never really end. For many of us, we may end up in a rat race that we can't get out of because of the payments and loans that we have already ended up committing to. The things we buy have a direct impact on the obligations that have to maintain.

Next, we have to worry about finding a partner, marriage, starting a family, buying a house, providing for your kids, setting aside money for their growth, college fund, the list goes on and on.

Do you feel overwhelmed with this summary of the first maybe one-third of your life? The reality is that that is probably the exact timeline that most of us will eventually go through. The next phase of life requires us to keep up the payments, to go to our jobs, to keep making that dough to sustain our family. We may have to also make enough money to pay for tuition fees, holidays, gifts, payments to parents, and whatever other commitments that we might have. And this might go on until we reach 60, when two-thirds of our lives are already behind us.

Life as you can see, without any external help, is already complicated enough. If you didn't already know by now, life isn't easy. Life is full of challenges, obligations, obstacles, commitments, and this is without any unforeseen events that might happen... Medical or family wise.

With all this in mind, why do we want to make life harder than it already is?

Every additional decision that you make on top of this list will only add to your burden, if it is not the right one, and every person that you add into your life that is negative will only bring the experience much less enjoyable.

To make life easier for you and your soul, I recommend that you choose each step wisely. Choose carefully the partner that you intend to spend your life with, choose wisely the people that you choose to spend your time with, choose wisely the food that you put in your body, and choose wisely the life that you wish to lead.

Be absolutely clear on the vision that you have for your life because it ain't easy.

Another thing to make your life much less complicated is to put less pressure on yourself. I believe that you don't need to start comparing your life with others because everyone is on their own journey. Don't chase the fancy houses and cars that your friends have just because they have them. Everyone is different and everyone's priorities might be different as well. They might pride having a luxury car over spending on other areas of life, which might differ from the interests that you might have. Comparison will only most certainly lead you to chase a life that you might not even want to attain. And you might lose your sleep and mind trying to match up to your peers. Focus on yourself instead and on exactly what you want out of life, and it will definitely be enough.

I challenge each and everyone of you to have a clear set of priorities for yourself. And once you have done so and are working towards those goals, be contented about it. Don't change the goalpost just because your friends say you must, or because you are jealous of what they have. Be satisfied in your own path and life will reward you with happiness as well.

Chapter 5:

Take Ownership of Yourself

What belongs to you but is used by other people more than you?
Your name.

And that's okay. People can use your name. But you must never allow yourself to lose ownership of you. In fact, you need to be incredibly conscious of taking ownership of everything that you are. And I do mean everything. Those few extra pounds, the nose you think is too big, your ginger hair or freckled skin. Whatever it is that you are insecure about, it's time that you showed up and took ownership. Because the moment you do your world will change.

But what does that look like? Why does it matter?

If someone parks a limo in the road outside your house, hands you the keys and tells you it is yours, what would you do? You're not just gonna put the keys in the ignition and leave it in the road. You are going to put that thing in a garage and get it insured. You will make sure that it is in a place where it is safe from weather and your jealous neighbour. Those are the things that you do when you take ownership of something. You make sure that they are protected because you value them. Then when you drive around town you don't look around as if you've stolen the thing. You drive with style and confidence. You are bold and comfortable because it belongs to you. *That* is what ownership looks like.

Now I know what you're thinking. That's easy to do with a limo, but I what I have is the equivalent of a car built before World War two. But the beautiful thing about ownership is that it does not depend on the object. It is not the thing being owned that you have to worry about, all you have to do is claim it. You've seen teenagers when they get their first car. Even if it is an old rust-bucket they drive around beaming with pride. Why? Because they know that what they have is theirs. It belongs to them and so they take ownership of it.

You have to do the same. You must take ownership of every part of you because in doing so you will keep it secure. You no longer have to be insecure about your weight if you know that that is where you are at right now. That doesn't mean you don't work for change though. It doesn't give you an excuse for stagnancy. You take accountability for your change and growth as much as you do for your present state. But in taking ownership you work towards polishing your pride, not getting rid of your low self-esteem. The difference may sound semantic, but the implications are enormous. The one allows you to work towards something and get somewhere good. The other makes it feel like you are just running away from something. And when you are running away then the only direction that matters is away – even if that means you run in circles.

Make a change today. Own yourself once more and be amazed at the rush that comes with it. With ownership comes confidence.

Chapter 6:

10 Signs of Teenage Depression

Teenage Depression is a difficult condition to identify as it may exhibit similar signs to normal teenage melancholia and moodiness. However, depression is a very serious condition that can have drastic effects on a teenager's developing personality and can lead to serious problems such as self-harm, substance misuse, educational breakdown, severe anxiety and suicide. Luckily, teenage depression it is a condition that responds well to treatment and can be greatly alleviated once identified and appropriate intervention secured. Teen years in general are a turbulent time. Occasional moodiness, irritability and acting out is therefore to be expected. However, depression is something different. Here the effect of sadness, anxiety and irritability can adversely affect the core of a teenager's personality.

10 Warning Signs Of Teenage Depression

1. Sadness and despair
2. Poor sense of self and self-belief
3. Anger and irritability
4. Tearfulness and crying
5. Social withdrawal & loss of interest in previously enjoyed activities

6. Changes in eating and sleeping patterns
7. Excessively harsh view of the self
8. Agitation or lack of motivation / boredom
9. Poor energy and concentration
10. Self-harm or Suicidal ideation

How Do I Know If It Is Teen Moodiness Or Teen Depression?

All of the above features exist on a spectrum. One must consider the severity and longevity of the above features to decide if it is a depressive episode or not. Dramatic changes in behaviour and personality are red flags for an emerging problem. Many young people who are attempting to cope with emotional distress will act out (externalize) via irritability, anger, school problems and moodiness whereas others will act in (internalizes) eating problems, withdrawal, low self esteem and secretive self harm.

How Does Teen Depression Differ From Depression In Adults?

Depression in teenagers is different to that of adults. Many consider depression to require the classic 'taking to the bed' and often adult depression may exhibit this feature. Teenage depression can be somewhat different. Sadness and social withdrawal may not always be a feature in fact anger, irritability and rage can be far more prominent. Teen depression also tends to be less pervasive, and many parents rule out adolescent depression because it appears that their child can appear not depressed when with their friends or on certain days. This lack of constancy is not necessarily a reason to exclude someone from the diagnosis. Other features that tend to be different in teenage depression to adult depression include increased irritability, psychosomatic or unexplained aches and pains, extreme sensitivity to criticism and unexplained withdrawal from activities.

Suicide And Depression

Suicide and depression although commonly linked are not always the case. Suicidal thoughts and behaviours can occur without a clear depressive episode and neither is a suicidal intent necessary for a depression diagnosis to be made. That said suicidal thoughts and urges are serious considerations for young people with depression. **Self-harm** behaviour is not always directly connected to suicidal intent. We must try to understand self-harm as an attempt to cope with emotional distress.

6 Warning Signs

1. Talk of suicide
2. Hopeless phrases like 'there is no point' 'I'd be better off dead'
3. Romanticizing death
4. Dark poetry, stories or drawings
5. Finalizing behaviour
6. Internet searches about suicide methods

How To Help

Talking therapies and medication are main treatments for teen depression but prior to this, parents and friends should offer support and be available to talk to the young person, be gentle but persistent, listen without lecturing, and validate young person's feelings.

Chapter 7:

6 Steps To Get Out of Your Comfort Zone

The year 2020 and 2021 have made a drastic change in all our lives, which might have its effect forever. The conditions of last year and a half have made a certain lifestyle choice for everyone, without having a say in it for us.

This new lifestyle has been a bit overwhelming for some and some started feeling lucky. Most of us feel comfortable working from home, and taking online classes while others want to have some access to public places like parks and restaurants.

But the pandemic has affected everyone more than once. And now we are all getting used to this relatively new experience of doing everything from home. Getting up every day to the same routine and the same environment sometimes takes us way back on our physical and mental development and creativity.

So, one must learn to leave the comfort zone and keep themselves proactive. Here are some ways anyone can become more productive and efficient.

Everyone is always getting ready to change but never changing.

1. Remember Your Teenage Self

People often feel nostalgic remembering those days of carelessness when they were kids and so oblivious in that teenage. But, little do they take for inspiration or motivation from those times. When you feel down, or when you don't feel like having the energy for something, just consider your teenage self at that time.

If only you were a teenager now, you won't be feeling lethargic or less motivated. Rather you'd be pushing harder and harder every second to get the job done as quickly as possible. If you could do it back then, you still can! All you need is some perspective and a medium to compare to.

2. Delegate Or Mentor Someone

Have you ever needed to have someone who could provide you some guidance or help with a problem that you have had for some time?

I'm sure, you weren't always a self-made man or a woman. Somewhere along the way, there was someone who gave you the golden quote that changed you consciously or subconsciously.

Now is the time for you to do the same for someone else. You could be a teacher, a speaker, or even a mentor who doesn't have any favors to ask in return. Once you get the real taste of soothing someone else's pain, you won't hesitate the next time.

This feeling of righteousness creates a chain reaction that always pushes you to get up and do good for anyone who could need you.

3. Volunteer In Groups

The work of volunteering may seem pointless or philanthropic. But the purpose for you to do it should be the respect that you might get, but the stride to get up on your feet and help others to be better off.

Volunteering for flood victims, earthquake affectees or the starving people of deserts and alpines can help you understand the better purpose of your existence. This keeps the engine of life running.

4. Try New Things For A Change

Remember the time in Pre-school when your teachers got you to try drawing, singing, acting, sculpting, sketching, and costume parties. Those weren't some childish approach to keep you engaged, but a planned system to get your real talents and skills to come out.

We are never too old to learn something new. Our passions are unlimited just as our dreams are. We only need a push to keep discovering the new horizons of our creative selves.

New things lead to new people who lead to new places which might lead to new possibilities. This is the circle of life and life is ironic enough to rarely repeat the same thing again.

You never know which stone might lead you to a gold mine. So never stop discovering and experiencing because this is what makes us the supreme being.

5. Push Your Physical Limits

This may sound cliched, but it always is the most important point of them all. You can never get out of your comfort zone, till you see the world through the hard glass.

The world is always softer on one side, but the image on the other side is far from reality. You can't expect to get paid equally to the person who works 12 hours a day in a large office of hundreds of employees. Only if you have the luxury of being the boss of the office.

You must push yourself to search for opportunities at every corner. Life has always more and better to offer at each stop, you just have to choose a stop.

6. Face Your Fears Once and For All

People seem to have a list of Dos and Dont's. The latter part is mostly because of a fear or a vacant thought that it might lead to failure for several reasons.

You need a "Do it all" behavior in life to have an optimistic approach to everything that comes in your way.

What is the biggest most horrible thing that can happen if you do any one of these things on your list? You need to have a clear vision of the possible worst outcome.

If you have a clear image of what you might lose, now must try to go for that thing and remove your fear once and for all. Unless you have something as important as your life to lose, you have nothing to fear from anything.

No one can force you to directly go skydiving if you are scared of heights. But you can start with baby steps, and then, maybe, later on in life you dare to take a leap of faith.

"Life is a rainbow, you might like one color and hate the other. But that doesn't make it ugly, only less tempting".

All you need is to be patient and content with what you have today, here, right now. But you should never stop aiming for more. And you certainly shouldn't regret it if you can't have or don't have it now.

People try to find their week spots and frown upon those moments of hard luck. What they don't realize is, that the time they wasted crying for what is in the past, could have been well spent for a far better future they could cherish for generations to come.

Chapter 8:

How To live Your Best Life

This is a simple yet not easy topic to tackle. But I am sure that this question is something that all of you are aspiring to achieve in life. Because really, being on earth, being alive, it does not have any real significance if we do not live it to our fullest potential, to enjoy every single wonderful thing that life has to offer, to smell the flowers, to see the sights along the way, and to appreciate the little things while going for the big dreams.

For many of us, I do believe that it was a lot easier to live our best life while we were in school. Whilst the pressure of school and getting good grades were always constantly hanging over us, that was the case for every other kid around us. It was fair game. And we all strived to be the best student that we could possibly be. At the same time, we had time to pursue our interests, learn new things, learn new skills, and even new instruments. The possibilities were endless, and the world was our oyster. We explored the deepest oceans and, in my opinion, we were indeed living our best lives as children and teens.

Making friends and hanging out with them frequently either through study or play weren't difficult. We were social creatures, and we were really good at that.

However, as we grew older, into our twenties and beyond, we start to lose that spark. That wonder. That curiosity. That vision that the world was in the palm of our hands. Instead, that view became more myopic, it keeps shrinking, work gets in the way, and we lose our sense of wonder and curiosity. We become more cynical and duller. And we stopped really trying to live our best life.

The introvert in us starts to come out more and more, and we retreat into our homes watching Netflix and YouTube, rather than going out there into the world and doing something significant or fun. In today's topic we are not going to talk about careers or income, because i do not believe that you need to be incredibly successful monetarily to be described as living your best life. But rather it's the other things that make up who you are that matters here.

And for many of us, it has become all too easy to retreat into the comfort of our home after a long day's work and decide that it is perfectly good to just lay on our couches and do nothing all day or weekend. We gradually disconnect ourselves from the outside world and we live in our own little bubble. And we think it is okay.

However, what we fail to realize is that over time, these hours add up to days, weeks, months, and even years. And we realize that at the end of it all, we have nothing to show for it. We have not put ourselves in positions where we are exposed to new experiences and things. Of fostering meaningful friendships that would last u to till the end of your life. And we find ourselves alone and regretting that we had not utilized our time more wisely to build up those relationships or creating those experiences that we can look back on and say I'm glad i did all those things. I'm glad i left no stone unturned. I'm glad i did not waste my time doing nothing.

So, to sum it all up, i believe that to live your best life, we should all look back at our middle school and high school days. What were we doing then that made everything so interesting and exciting, and how can we integrate more of that into our lives instead of choosing isolation? Whether that be trying out a new activity, learning a new sport, or even simply just hanging out with friends that you can rely on a much more regular basis. I do believe that you will start to feel that life has much more meaning, and happiness will soon follow.

Chapter 9:

Becoming a Leader

Wow today we're going to talk about a topic that i think might not apply to everybody but it is one that is definitely interesting as well and good for everyone to know if they someday aspire to be a leader of sorts.

Leadership is something that does not come naturally to everyone, while some are born leaders as they say, in reality most of us requires life experiences, training, and simply good people skills in order to be an effective leader that is respected.

To be a respected leader, you have to have excellent communication skills who come across as fair and just to your employees while also being able to make tough decisions when the time comes.

I believe that leaders are not born, but their power is earned. A person who has not had the opportunities to deal with others on a social and business level can never be able to make effective decisions that serves the well being of others. A leader in any organization is one that is able to command respect not by force but by implicit authority.

So what are some ways that you can acquire leadership skills if you feel that you lack experience in it? Well first of all I believe that putting yourself in more social and group settings in friendly situations is a good place to start. Instead of jumping right into a work project, you can start by organizing an activity where you are in charge. For example, those that involve team work and team games. Maybe an escape room, or even simply taking charge by organizing a party and planning an event where you become the host, and that usually means that you are in charge of getting things in order and all the nitty gritty stuff. Planning parties, coordinating people, time management, giving instructions, preparing materials... All these little pieces require leadership to pull off. And with these practices in events that will not affect your professional career, after you get a good feel of what it is like, you can move on to taking on a leadership role in projects at school or work. And hopefully over time all these practices will add up and you will be a much more holistic leader.

Soft skills are a key part to being an effective leader as well. Apart from professional expertise at the workplace. So I encourage you to be as proficient in your learning of people skills and mastering interpersonal communication as well as being fluent in all the intricacies and details of your job description.

If you require a higher level of leadership training, i would encourage you to sign up for a course that would put you in much more challenging situations where you will be put to the test. This may be the push that you need to get you on your path to be the leader that you always thought that you could be.

Personally, I have always been a leader, not of a team, but of my own path. That instead of following in the footsteps of someone, or taking orders from bosses, i like to take charge of what I do with my time. And how to manage my career in that fashion. As much as I would like to tell myself that i am an effective leader, more often that not, I can honestly say i wish i was better. I wish I was better at managing my time, at managing my finances, at managing my work, and I have to always upgrade my leadership skills to ensure that I am effective in what I do. That I do not waste precious time.

Your leadership goals might be different from mine. Maybe you have an aspiration to be a head of a company, or division, or to lead a group in charitable work, or to be a leader of a travel tour group. Being a leader comes in all forms and shapes, and your soft skills can definitely by transferable in all areas.

So I challenge you to take leadership seriously and to think of ways to improve your leadership skills by placing yourself in situations where you can fine tune every aspect of your personality when dealing with others. At the end of the day, how people perceive you may be the most important factor of all.

Chapter 10:

Become A High Performer

We were put on this planet because we were meant to be all we could become. Human beings are the sum of their acts and achievements. But not everyone is capable of doing things to their full potential.

Every man's biggest burden is his or her unfulfilled potential.

So what you need to become a high-performing individual in this modern era of competition is to idolize the best of the best.

You will need to understand the real-life features of a successful individual and what you need to do to become one.

If you want to be more successful in your life you need to become obsessive. Start your day with a goal and try your best to achieve it before you head to bed. You don't necessarily need to be on the right path with the first step, but you will find the best route once you have the undefeated will to find that path.

If you want to be more developed in your life you need to sleep effectively. The most successful people have a mantra of high performing routine. They don't sleep more than five hours a day and work seven days a week. They only take one day a week to sleep more just to rejuvenate their brains and body.

If you want to know if you are a high-performing successful person, look into your body language. If you find ease and leisure in everyday tasks, You are surely not standing up to your potential. If you like to sit for a conversation, start to stand. If you like to walk, start running. Get out of your comfort zone and start thinking and acting differently.

The last thing before you start your search for the right path to excellence is to set a goal every day. Increase your creativity by finding new ways to shorten the time of you becoming the better you and finally getting what you deserve.

You will eventually start seeing your life get on the track of productive learning and execution.

Change your way of treating others, especially those who are below you. If you are not a jolly person when you are broke, you can never be a jolly person when you are rich.

Never underestimate someone who is below you. You never know to whom the inspiration might take you. You have to consider the fact that life is ever-changing. Nothing ever stays the same. People never stay where they are for long.

It is the alternating nature of life that makes you keep fighting and pushing harder for better days. That is why you work hard on your skills to become a hearty human with the arms of steel.

Most people live a quiet life of desperation where they have a lot to give and a lot to say but can never get out of their cocoons.

But you are not every other person. You are the most unique soul god has created to excel at something no one has ever thought or seen before.

Start loving yourself. Stop finding faults in yourself. You are the best version of yourself, you just haven't found the right picture to look into it yet.

You want to be a high performer in every aspect of your life, here is my final advice for you.

If you push your limits in even the smallest tasks of your life, if you stretch your mind and imagination, if you can push the rules to your benefit, you might be the happiest and the most successful man humankind has ever seen.

Keep working for your dreams till the day you die. Life opens its doors to the people who knock on it. The purpose of this life is to knock on every door of opportunity and grasp that opportunity before anyone else steps forward.

You won't fulfill your desires till you make the desired effort, and that comes with a strong will and character. So keep doing what you want to never have a regret.

Chapter 11:

Becoming High Achievers

By becoming high achievers, we become high off life, what better feeling is there than aiming for something you thought was unrealistic and then actually hitting that goal.

What better feeling is there than declaring we will do something against the perceived odds and then actually doing it.

To be a high achiever you must be a believer,

You must believe in yourself and believe that dream is possible for you.

It doesn't matter what anyone else thinks, as long as you believe,

To be a high achiever we must hunger to achieve.

To be an action taker.

Moving forward no matter what.

High achievers do not quit.

Keeping that vision in their minds eye until it becomes reality, no matter what.

Your biggest dream is protected by fear , loss and pain.

We must conquer all 3 of these impostors to walk through the door.

Not many do, most are still fighting fear and if they lose the battle, they quit.

Loss and pain are part of life.

Losses are hard on all of us.

Whether we lose possessions, whether we lose friends, whether we lose our jobs, or whether we lose family members.

Losing doesn't mean you have lost.

Losses are may be a tough pill to swallow, but they are essential because we cannot truly succeed until we fail.

We can't have the perfect relationship if we stay in a toxic one, and we can't have the life we desire until we make room by letting go of the old.

The 3 imposters that cause us so much terror are actually the first signs of our success.

So walk through fear in courage, look at loss as an eventual gain, and know that the pain is part of the game and without it you would be weak.

Becoming a high achiever requires a single-minded focus on your goal, full commitment and an unnatural amount of persistence and work.

We must define what high achievement means to us individually, set the bar high and accept nothing less.

The achievement should not be money as money is not our currency but a tool.

The real currency is time, and your result is the time you get to experience the world's places and products, so the result should always be that.

The holiday home, the fast car and the lifestyle of being healthy and wealthy, those are merely motivations to work towards. Like Carrots on a stick.

High achievement is individual to all of us, it means different things to each of us,

But if we are going to go for it we might as well go all out for the life we want, should we not?

I don't think we beat the odds of 1 in 400 trillion to be born, just to settle for mediocrity, did we?

Being a high achiever is in your DNA, if you can beat the odds, you can beat anything.

It is all about self-belief and confidence, we must have the confidence to take the action required and often the risk.

Risk is difficult for people and it's a difficult tight rope to walk. The line between risk and recklessness is razor thin.

Taking risks feels unnatural, not surprisingly as we all grew up in a health and safety bubble with all advice pointing towards safe and secure ways.

But the reward is often in the risk and sometimes a leap of blind faith is required. This is what stops most of us - the fear of the unknown.

The truth is the path to success is foggy and we can only ever see one step ahead, we have to imagine the result and know it's somewhere down this foggy path and keep moving forward with our new life in mind.

Know that we can make it but be aware that along the path we will be met by fear, loss and pain and the bigger our goal the bigger these monsters will be.

The top achievers financially are fanatical about their work and often work 100+ hours per week.

Some often work day and night until a project is successful.

Being a high achiever requires giving more than what is expected, standing out for the high standard of your work because being known as number 1 in your field will pay you abundantly.

Being an innovator, thinking outside the box for better practices, creating superior products to your competition because quality is more rewarding than quantity.

Maximizing the quality of your products and services to give assurance to your customers that your company is the number 1 choice.

What can we do differently to bring a better result to the table and a better experience for our customers?

We must think about questions like that because change is inevitable and without thinking like that we get left behind, but if we keep asking that, we can successfully ride the wave of change straight to the beach of our desired results.

The route to your success is by making people happy because none of us can do anything alone, we must earn the money and to earn it we must make either our employers or employees and customers happy.

To engage in self-promotion and positive interaction with those around us, we must be polite and positive with everyone, even with our competition.

Because really the only competition is ourselves and that is all we should focus on.

Self-mastery, how can I do better than yesterday?

What can I do different today that will improve my circumstances for tomorrow?

Little changes add up to a big one.

The belief and persistence towards your desired results should be 100%, I will carry on until… is the right attitude.

We must declare to ourselves that we will do this, we don't yet know how but we know that we will.

Because high achievers like yourselves know that to make it you must endure and persist until you win.

High achievers have an unnatural grit and thick skin, often doing what others won't, putting in the extra hours when others don't.

After you endure loss and conquer pain, the sky is the limit, and high achievers never settle until they are finished.

Chapter 12:

Believe in Yourself

Listen up. I want to tell you a story. This story is about a boy. A boy who became a man, despite all odds. You see, when he was a child, he didn't have a lot going for him. The smallest and weakest in his class, he had to struggle every day just to keep up with his peers. Every minute of every hour was a fight against an opponent bigger and stronger than he was - and every day he was knocked down. Beaten. Defeated. But... despite that... despite everything that was going against him... this small, weak boy had one thing that separated him from hundreds of millions of people in this world. A differentiating factor that made a difference in the matter of what makes a winner in this world of losers. You see this boy believed in himself. No matter the odds, he believed fundamentally that he had the power to overcome anything that got in his way! It didn't matter how many times he was knocked down, he got RIGHT BACK UP!

Now it wasn't easy. It hurt like hell. Every time he failed was another reminder of how far behind he was. A reminder of the nearly insurmountable gap between him and everyone else and lurking behind that reminder was the temptation, the suggestion to just give up. Throw in the towel. Surrender the win. Yet believe me when I tell you that no matter HOW tough things got, no matter HOW much he wanted to give in, a small voice in his heart keep saying... not today... just once more... I know it hurts but I can try again... Just. Once. More.

You see more than anything in this world HE KNEW that deep inside him was a greatness just WAITING to be tapped into! A power that most people would never see, but not him. It didn't matter what the world threw at him, because he'd be damned if he let his potential die alongside him. And all it took? All it required to unlock the chasm of greatness inside was a moment to realize the lies the world tried to tell him. In less than a second, he recognized the light inside that would ignite a spark of success to address the ones who didn't believe that he could do it. The ones who told him to give up! Get out! Go home and roam the streets where failure meets those who weren't born to sit at the seat at the top!

Yet what they didn't know is that being born weak didn't matter any longer 'cause in his fight to succeed he became stronger. Rising up to the heights beyond, he WOULD NOT GIVE UP till he forged a bond within his heart that ensured NO MATTER THE ODDS, no matter what anyone said about him, no matter what the world told him, he had something that NO ONE could take away from him. A power so strong it transformed this boy into a man. A loser into a winner. A failure into a success. That, is the power of self-belief...

Chapter 13:

Block Out The Critics and Detractors

There is drama everywhere around us. In fact, our whole life is a drama. A drama that has more complex turns and thrillers than the best thriller ever to be made on a cinema screen.

This drama isn't always a result of our own actions. Sometimes we do something stupid to contribute towards anarchy. But mostly the things happening around us seem to be a drama because the critics make a hell out of everything.

We get sucked into things that and someone else's opinions because we do not know what we are doing.

It may sound cliche but remember that it doesn't matter what anyone else says. In fact, most discoveries and inventions got bad press when they were found or made. It was only after they are gone when people actually came to appreciate the true importance of those inventions.

The time will come sooner or later when you are finally appreciated for your work and your effort. But your work should not depend on what others will say.

Your work should not depend on the hope of appreciation or the fear of criticism, rather it should be done because it was meant to be done. You should put your heart and soul in it because you had a reason for all this and only you will reap the fruit, no matter what the world gets from it.

You don't need to do the best out there in the world and neither should you be judged on that standard. But you should put out the best YOU can do because that will someday shut out the critics as they start to see your true potential.

The work itself doesn't matter, but the effort you put behind it does. You don't need to be an insult to anyone who mocks you or criticizes you on even your best work. Empathy is your best approach to bullying.

You cannot possibly shut out every critic. You spend your whole life trying to answer to those meaningless least important people that weren't even able to make their own lives better. Because those who did make something of themselves didn't find it worthwhile to distract and degrade everyone else.

So, you should try to spend your time more and more on your good work. Keep a straight sight without even thinking to look at one more ordinary critic who doesn't give a simple feeling of empathy towards your efforts.

You only need to put yourself in others' shoes and look at yourself through their eyes. If you can do that before them, you would have the best reply to any hurtful comment. And that my friend will be true silence.

People always come to gather around you when they see a cause they can relate to. So, give them a cause. Give a ray of hope and motivation to people around you and you will finally get to get the critics on your side.

Your critics will help you get to the top from the hardest side there is.

Chapter 14:

Bounce Back From Failure

Failure is a big word. It is a negative word most say. It is cursed in most cases. It is frowned upon when it is on your plate. But why?

Sure, it certainly doesn't feel good when you encounter failure. We can't even forgive ourselves for failing at a simple card game. We get impatient, we get hopeless and ultimately we get depressed on even the smallest of failure we go through in everyday life.

Why is it that way? Why can't we try to change a failure into something better? Why can't we just leave that failure right there and not try to make a big deal out of each and every small little setback?

These questions have a very deep meaning and a very important place in everyone's life.

Let's start with the simplest step to make it easy for yourself to deal with a certain failure. Whenever you fail at anything, just pause for a second and talk to yourself.

Rewind what you just went through. Talk to yourself through the present circumstances. Think about what you could have done to improve at what you just did. Think about what you could have done to prevent whatever tragic incident you went through. Or what you could have done to do better at what you felt like failing at.

These questions will immediately sketch a scenario in front of your eyes. A scenario where you can actually see yourself flourishing and doing your best against all odds.

Whatever happened to you, I am sure you didn't deserve it. But so, what if you lost some money or a loved one or your pet? Ask yourself this, is it the end of the world? Have you stopped breathing? Have you no reason left to keep living?

You had, you have, and you will always have a new thing, a new person a new place to start with. Life has endless possibilities for you to find. But you just have to bounce back from whatever setback you think you cannot get out of.

Take for example the biggest tech billionaires in the world. I am giving this example because people tend to relate more to these examples these days. Elon Musk started his carrier with a small office with his brother and they both lived in the same office for a whole year. They couldn't even afford a small place for themselves to rent.

There was a time when Elon had to decide to split his last set of investments between two companies. If he had invested in one, the other would have gone down for sure, just to give a chance to the other company to maybe become their one big hit. Guess what, he ended up keeping them both because he invested in both.

Why did he succeed? Was it because he wasn't afraid? No!

He succeeded because he had Faith after all the failures he had faced. He knew that if he kept trying against all odds and even the obvious risks, he will ultimately succeed at something for what he worked so hard for all this time!

Chapter 15:

Building Confidence

The things we strive for all our lives are a mere image of what we can achieve and what we want to achieve.

There is a difference between two very important aspects of our life. One is self-esteem and the other is self-confidence. You have very high self-esteem if you think big of yourself and have respect for your craft. This is a very important thing to have because no one is big on confidence if they don't have a good opinion about themselves.

We often say that 'You and You only are your best critic'. This isn't a statement for the narrow-minded.

If you think big of yourself, you will have a better perspective of the things you do and wish to do someday. If you have a 'No Go' confidence towards everything, then you have nothing to start with.

Do you want to build confidence? Take some tips, just as a piece of advice.

If you want to build confidence, focus on what you can't do, not on what you can't. I know this is against everything we think someone will say to boost your morale.

But the truth is, that when you start to work on things that you cannot do, you will try it for some time, but then you will eventually fail. That might prove to be a breaking point for some people.

If you focus on what you can do, you will always be successful. And you will praise your good work, and that will help you every time exponentially. The more you proceed, the more you will succeed and the more you will be confident in yourself.

You also need to surround yourself with people who believe in you.

Every person in his life has had a moment when they were just about to summit the biggest achievement of their life. But gave up or lost hope because they let the noise and opinions around them get into their heads.

Those who have opinions have nothing else going on in their lives. So, they try to mend their souls by inflicting negation on others. You don't have time or energy to deal with these people.

So, keep the people in your life who have the same approach towards life as you and they love you for who you are. These people will help you in even the darkest deepest days of your life.

The last piece of advice is what we have heard from the first step that we took in our childhood. The advice of never giving up!

You will fail here and there everywhere in your life. You are meant to fail. Everyone is meant to fail someday. But you cannot give up! You Should Never Give Up!

We have a lot of things going on in our lives and one or the other is meant to fall apart someday. We lose money. We lose friends. We lose family. But what you cannot lose forever is Hope.

Till the day you have hope, you have a reserve to keep you on the track and maybe someday, fly like a phoenix.

Chapter 16:

Confidence: The Art of Humble-Pride

There is a very fine line between confidence and overconfidence, being bold and being belligerent, having authority and having arrogance. It is a line that trips even the most nimble footed, but usually because they have dedicated no clear thoughts on how to manage it. Instead, they follow their gut on how far they can push or how much they should hold back.

This is the paradox; you need to be confident. You need self-belief, you need to be assured of your ability and sometimes even certain of what the outcome will be. All of those things are empowering. In the words of Tony Robbins, you have to awaken the giant within. But had Goliath stooped to consider David's sling he would have worn a different helmet. The problem was that Goliath had a belief that he was fully capable of everything just as he was. I like to call it confidence without context, or universal, unanimous support of the self. That is the dangerous kind of confidence that spills over into arrogance. Chess grandmasters will tell you that the moment you assume you will win is the moment you lose. Because that is precisely when you start to make mistakes. You become too focussed on what your next move is that you don't even see theirs.

You become so absorbed in your strategy that you fail to account for their plan and the bigger picture. It was confidence without context that made Goliath run straight towards to the flying stone.

Confidence without context is an assumption. And the problem with assumptions is that they go one step beyond the rationality of an expectation. Assumption goes into the fight drunk, having already celebrated the victory. But that leads to its inevitable demise. Expectation remains present, it acknowledges the reality of the situation. Assumption arrives intoxicated, expectation arrives in control. That is the difference.

Pride is the greatest antidote to reason, which makes humility its greatest ally. If you want to stay in the fight you need to have both confidence and humility. If you want to stay competitive, if you want to get a promotion, if you want to level up. Whatever it is that you want, I can guarantee that the path to get there is a hopscotch of humility and confidence. Every bold step forward must be followed by a humble one. Note that humility does not take you backwards, it keeps you balanced. You can hop along in arrogance, but you will never last as long or be as strong as the one who keeps an even stride. If you strive for something, then you need to start striding towards it. And the rhythm of your march should beat to the sounds of a two-tone drum. Because confidence without context is like hopping up stairs – you might reach the second floor, but you will never manage the pyramid.

Chapter 17:

Change Your Environment For Success

Human life resembles a lot of things. Take leaves of a tree for example. Leaves change color throughout the year. Ever thought why does it happen?

Trees change the color of their leaves to adapt to the different seasons, preparing for what is coming ahead of them.

It is not exclusive only to plants. A lot of animals also have different approaches towards different climatic changes. A lot of polar birds migrate thousands of miles due South, just before the winter season comes in. A lot of fish move to warm waters in the fall season.

Ever wondered why? Because they want o make sure the survival of their species and they want to provide a habitat for their of-springs where they can flourish and nourish well.

Do you want to be a successful human being? You should make a stronger network with your species. The more you interact with your species the more you are to have a better social life, the better chances you have at learning, and the better chances of survival you have if you have someone dependable to rely on.

The effects your environment and your company have on you will determine how pessimistic, ambitious, and or organized you are. You will feel the change in the course of events just as you start to make a change in your environment.

Every man needs a productive and nourishing environment to flourish to his or her full limits. And maybe even push the limits further.

You also need to realize that whatever you are in search of will always be achievable, but you have to make a routine and a habitat where you can relax when you are feeling low.

Most of us take our health for granted. We take our sleep for granted and a disruptive sleep cycle can change our behavior. If you don't have a good place to sleep and if you don't have a nice comfortable bed or bedding to curl up in, you will not be able to restore all your creative juices.

These juices will only flow when you will let them, and for that, you need to create a window of the calming and soothing environment to sleep in.

Now if you have a goal and you know the right path to it, stay put and start by bringing in the most relevant things nearer to you. Start pushing the unnecessary thins out of your habitat and you will be forwarding one step closer to success.

We don't realize this fully but we are truly a product of our environment and our relationships.

Every new day is a new chance to bring a change in our lives. Find new things that inspire you. Find New people that motivate you. Find newer things that push you. Find better goals that make you shine bigger and better than everyone else around you.

If you are willing to change what you love the most around you, you are already far ahead on your path to success.

Chapter 18:

Changing How You Think

The Powerhouse Of The Body

Just like every car has an engine and mobile phones have batteries, so does the human body have the mind. It is the powerhouse of the body. Despite its small physical size, the power of the brain should not be underestimated.

The brain conceives an idea, considers its viability before it transforms it into an innovation. You are assured of a brighter future if you have a sober mind.

This vital function of the mind makes it a gem. It should be protected at all costs and well nurtured for the best results. Your thinking pattern is a result of the state of your mind.

The Environment Factor

The environment affects the functioning of your brain, thinking, and reaction to many issues. Be wary of your environment. The performance of academically bright students can reduce when they change schools from high-ranking ones to lesser ones. This proven fact is evidence of the impact of the environment you are in.

What distinguishes the rich from the poor is how they think. The mind brings the difference in their lives. Once-upon-a-time friends can part ways based on their thinking habits. At some point, one even changes their residence. They no longer feel secure mingling with people whom they do not think alike.

Thinking Patterns

There are divergent thinking patterns based on many factors. Apart from the environment, one's personality has a major role in determining how one thinks. Individual personality traits determine your shift in thinking behaviors.

Introverts and extroverts differ in thinking because of their different traits. One would take his time before deciding while another will decide at the moment. This does not make either of them right or wrong.

To successfully change how you think, you should first classify yourself correctly in the category you fall. If you are having a problem, consult a more experienced friend who shall be honest with you.

This is how you can change your thinking patterns based on your personality traits:

1. Social Exposure

Do you travel often? Or do you love making friendships with strangers? This is very important when you want to shift your thinking habits. While introverts enjoy their own company, extroverts love new experiences. They are outgoing and easily make new friends.

As an introvert, try being outgoing for some time. Make new friends apart from those you are comfortable with. This does not mean you should change your personality but you should accommodate a different approach.

New friends will challenge your traditional thinking approach. They will inspire you to do things differently to obtain different results. However, be careful not to be carried away by popular opinion. Always seek to maintain your independence.

On the other hand, if you are extroverted, try minimizing external influence in your decisions. You are prone to thinking like your peers because you easily absorb new practices. Take some time to withdraw from the crowd. This retreat will make you see the blind spots that you cannot see when you are with your friends.

2. Education And Life Skills

Ignorance is the reason why many people make poor decisions. It is important to be enlightened because you will not fall into the traps that ensnare many. Education – formal, informal, or both – is light to our paths.

One thing about education is that we learn from the mistakes of other people instead of our own. When our turn comes, we can evade their mistakes. Through education, we walk in the footsteps of great people and become like them. Our thinking patterns can largely be influenced by our mentors.

Life skills sharpen our minds and teach us ways how we can face challenges. Although challenges mutate with time and become sophisticated, life skills help us to brave them. Do not despise life skills as part of informal learning, they are important in changing our initial perspective of things

In conclusion, changing how you think requires time to learn and effort to implement. It also needs a ready mind to try new things that will be impactful in their lives. Take the bold step today!

Chapter 19:

Contribute To Society In A Meaningful Way

Today we are going to talk about how and why you should do work that contributes to society in a meaningful way. And the benefits that it can bring to all aspects of your life, be it psychological, sociological, or physical.

Why do I feel that this topic is of importance that I should highlight it in today's episode? Well because if there is one thing i have noticed about my salaried friend workers around me, I do feel that they lack a bigger vision and purpose for their life. And i feel that there is a sense that the end goal of their work is not to the benefit of their own personal growth, but of the $ sign at the end. And this motivation to work towards a 5 figure pay check is one that ultimately brings not much joy and meaning to one's life.

The many friends that I have interviewed have told me repeatedly that these jobs are merely a means to an end. That it's a routine that they have pretty much resigned themselves to sustain a lifestyle that they feel is good enough for them. This mentality has gotten me to question the culture of whether a monetary goal is truly sufficient in making one truly happy. Yes to an extent, money can bring about freedom which would free up time for one to pursue their passions in life, but for most, this race towards $10k just feels futile.

I would argue that only when you know what to do with freedom of time, and that is to serve a purpose greater than your own selfish needs, can you truly have a meaningful time on this earth.

The greatest entrepreneurs today make their millions not by chasing the money per se, but rather by finding problems that they can solve. They find a gap in society, a need that needs to be filled, and invent a novel solution to a problem that aims to address those holes. Think Jeff Bezos, Steve Jobs, Elon Musk, Mark Zuckerberg. These billionaires have their customers and consumers in mind when they set out to create their mega companies that have largely dominated our world today.

Now I am not saying you need to be doing these crazy big deals to live a happy life, but i believe that everyone has an ability to start somewhere, to start small in our community. If you have no desire for entrepreneurship and are contented with being a salaried worker, that is absolutely perfect. However, you can consider doing some volunteer work, and working with a community that can better the lives of someone out there even if it just by a little bit. I guarantee that these selfless acts of giving your time to help someone out in your unique way will reward you with a feeling that money just can't buy.

If you feel like you can do more, you can dedicate more of your time to a particular cause that resonates with you, that you will not feel like a chore to serve. A cause that strikes your heart and soul that makes you want to go back so that you can give more and do more.

Maybe this cause will be something you might end up dedicating your life to, you never know. But I do know that chasing money and dedicating your life to making money will never make you happy. Invest in others, invest in their spirit, invest in doing good for society will be infinitely more worthy of your time and energy.

I challenge you today to see in what areas can you contribute to society and do good for others. I believe that you will not only feel purpose, but it will help sustain you in your career and work as well, giving you a fresh perspective on what life is really all about.

Chapter 20:

Dealing with Career Pressure

Dealing with pressure related to work is A very difficult thing to achieve. People deal with career-related pressures daily. Be it A job or A business or even studies. In the fast-evolving world of today, people often forget about their own mental and physical health because of the immense pressures of work and the environment. There are many things that you can do to lower this pressure and become more productive.

The first thing to do is to stay calm. This is not an easy thing to do but is very effective. Staying positive under pressure can help you to stay calm and complete the task at hand. To stay positive, A person should always be optimistic and should always believe that they can complete the task under pressure. The next goal is to stay focused on the task. One should always let go of thoughts that are getting in the way of their work and slowing them down. Staying focused helps you to achieve your goals before the deadline. This is one step closer to self-appreciation, which is very helpful in situations where the pressure is high. Another way of reducing pressure is to stay away from any arguments within the organization because getting engaged in them can lead to stress and wasting your own time.

On the other hand, if you are not engaging in arguments, your reputation within the organization can become better, and sometimes employees that are loyal to the organization get easier tasks as compared to employees that are causing trouble. Asking for help is always A way of reducing pressure. A task can be achieved much quicker if A bunch of people are working together. This is why workgroups are formed within an organization because they increase efficiency. Asking for help is never bad, and one must not be ashamed of doing so. Utilizing your holidays for your betterment can lead to reducing work-related pressure and stress. Lastly, people who rely on coffee and chocolate snacks should limit their intake because these are stimulants. Taking them in a small amount is fine but drinking too much coffee or eating too much chocolate snacks can cause undue stress and restlessness, which can make the already stressful situation even worse.

There are A lot of seminars and activities to help you perform better under pressure. Joining them can be very beneficial for A person who is having difficulties in these areas. Choosing the right career for yourself is also better because if A person is doing what they enjoy, there is very little pressure because they are having A good time. On the other hand, if A person chooses A career that is not made for them, however good they are at it, A time will come when they will be questioning their decision, and they won't be able to do anything about it. Proper career counselling can be very helpful, and everyone should seek it before opting for A career. These experts evaluate A person and help them to choose the right career which they can perform better and be happy with their job. Finding A career that suits you best and working hard towards it will ensure your success. Getting pressured about choosing the right career is common, but as long as you are satisfied with what you choose, you are good to go!

Chapter 21:

Dealing With Addictions

People engaging in addictive behavior go on to develop an actual addiction. They find that overcoming it is more challenging than they had expected. Most people believe that addiction is A myth and they can quit any time they want to, or they feel that they are an exception to the rule. It's only when they have completely fallen into the trap do they find themselves completely screwed. This is more likely with non-substance or behavioural addictions like - excessive eating, sex, gambling, shopping, and even exercise. What makes it more harmful and complicated is that for every addictive behaviour, some people can engage in the behaviour without developing an addiction.

Most people think that they are one of the lucky few who won't get hooked. But unfortunately, they don't realize the truth until it's too late. By the time they recognize the need for change, they may not even want to. It takes years of being faced with the negative consequences of an addiction before realizing that it might be causing significant problems.

Sooner or later, most people who have an addiction should decide that A change is necessary. Once they have made the decision and set up A specific goal in their mind, like quitting entirely or quitting only A portion of it from time to time, they can get A head start to work in that direction.

Getting clear on your goal before putting it into practice is helpful for success in overcoming your addictions. Although quitting entirely may be the best path to wellness, reducing or eliminating the most harmful substances first is still A huge improvement and will greatly reduce the harm caused.

Once you get clear on your goal, you are still asked to prepare yourself for the change. Preparations might include removing addictive substances from your home and work, as well as eliminating any triggers in your life that may ensure you use those substances again. Suddenly quitting an addictive behaviour can be lonely, especially when you lose touch with people who don't indulge in the same behaviours. Take out time to contact friends and family who will support you in your goals without being judgemental. Find people who will take care of you when you slip up. Lose all those negative friends with whom you drink, use drugs, or engage in any addictive behaviours.

Quitting an addictive behaviour is never easy, and there is no right way to feel while you are quitting. You will feel like going back to your old habits, and you will find yourself depressed and cut off from the world. But that's okay. Give yourself time and re-evaluate yourself. If you start to feel like this, all is too overwhelming for you, and you can try different treatments that can help you to overcome your addiction. They can either be medical or psychological. There is no right type of treatment, and you have to decide for yourself which treatment is suiting you best. Cognitive behaviour therapy (cbt) helps many people. Research shows it is quite effective in helping people to deal with and overcome all kinds of addictions. You can also always consult A psychologist/psychiatrist to discuss your thoughts and seek medications.

Long-term recovery is an ongoing process of facing and coping with life without retreating into addictive behaviours. It's not the final destination. Seek help when you need it. Be proud of yourself and understand that you have come A long way and still have A long way to go.

Chapter 22:

Dealing With Addiction To Technology

Today we're going to talk about addiction to technology and media consumption. I think this is a topic that many of us can relate, even myself included. Am my goal for today is to try to help put forth a more sustainable and healthy habit for you to still enjoy technology while not being overwhelmed and overtaken by it completely.

So, let's ask ourselves a simple question of why are we so hooked into using our devices so frequently and sparingly? I think for most of us, and this is my personal opinion, is that it offers us an escape, a distraction from our everyday tasks that we know we ought to do. To procrastinate just a little bit or to binge scroll on Instagram, Facebook, Snapchat, and what have you, to satisfy our need for media consumption.

We use technology as a tool a gateway into the world of digital media, and we get lost in it because companies try to feed us with posts and stuff that we like to keep us engaged and to keep us watching just a little while longer. And minutes can turn into hours, and before you know it, it is bedtime.

I want to argue that this addiction is not entirely your fault, but that these multi billion dollar mega companies are being fed so much data that they are able to manipulate us into consume their media. It is like how casinos use various tricks of flickering lights, and free drinks to keep you playing a little longer and to spend a little more of your attention and time. We unknowingly get subjected to these manipulative tactics, and we fall for it despite our best efforts to abstain from it.

I for one have been the subject of such manipulation. Whether it be Netflix or my favourite social media apps, I find myself mindlessly scrolling through posts trying to get my quick fix of distraction and supposed stress relief. However, these feelings don't bring me joy, rather it brings me anxiety that I have wasted precious time and I end up kicking myself for it afterwards. This happens time and time again and it felt like I was stuck in a loop, unable to get out.

So, what is the solution to this seemingly endless spiral of bad habits? Some might say just to delete the apps or turn off wifi. But how many of you might have actually tried that yourself only to have it backfire on you? Redownloading the app is only one step away, wifi is only one button away, and addictions aren't so easily kicked to the curb as one might think.

What I have found that works is that instead of consuming mindless media that don't bring about actual benefit to my life, I chose to watch content that I could actually learn something from. Like this channel for example. I went on the hunt to seek out content that I could learn how to make extra money, how to improve my health, how to improve my relationships, basically anything that had to do with personal development. And I found that I actually felt less guilty watching or reading these posts even though they still do take up my time to consume.

You may call it a lesser of two evils, but what I discovered was that it provided much more benefit to my life than actually not consuming any personal development media at all. Whether it be inspirational stories from successful entrepreneurs like Elon Musk, or Jeff Bezos, or multi billion-dollar investment advice from Warren Buffet, these passive watching of useful content actually boosted my knowledge in areas that I might otherwise have not been exposed to. Subconsciously, i started internalizing some of these beliefs and adopted it into my own psyche. And i transformed what was mindless binge watching of useless Tv shows and zombie content, to something that actually moved the needle in my life in the right direction, even by a little.

Overtime, I actually required less and less distraction of media consumption using my technology devices like iPhones and iPads or Macs and started putting more attention and effort to do the work that I knew I had to get done. Because some of these personal development videos actually taught me what I needed to do to get stuff done and to stop procrastinating in working towards my goals.

So, I challenge each and everyone of you today to do a thorough review of the kinds of music and media consumption that you consume today with your smartphones and tablets and see if you can substitute them with something that you can learn from, no matter how trivial you think it may be. It could be the very push you need to start porting over all your bad habits of technology into something that can pay off for you 10 years down the road.

Chapter 23:

Dealing With Difficult People

It is inevitable that people will rub us the wrong way as we go about our days. Dealing with such people requires a lot of patience and self-control, especially if they are persistent in their actions towards you over a lengthy period of time.

Difficult people are outside the realm of our control and hence we need to implement strategies to deal with negative emotions should they arise. If you encounter such people frequently, here are 7 ways that you can take back control of the situation.

1. Write Your Feelings Down Immediately

A lot of times we bottle up feelings when someone is rude or unpleasant to us. We may have an urge to respond but in the moment, we choose not to. In those circumstances, the next best thing we can do is to write down our feelings either in our journals or in our smartphones as notes.

Writing our feelings down is a therapeutic way to cleanse our thoughts and negative energy. In writing we can say the things we wished we had said and find out the reasons that made us feel uneasy in the first place.

In writing we are also able to clearly identify the trigger points and could work backwards in managing our expectations and feelings around the person. If it is a rude customer, or a rude stranger, we may not be able to respond for fear or retaliation or for fear of losing our jobs. It is best those situations not to erupt in anger but take the time to work through those emotions in writing.

2. Tell The Person Directly What You Dislike About Their Attitude

If customer service and retail isn't your profession, or if it is not your boss, you may have the power to voice your opinion directly to the person who wronged you. If confrontation is something that you are comfortable with, don't hesitate to express to them why you are dissatisfied with their treatment or attitude towards you. You may also prefer to clear your head before coming back to confront the person and not let emotions escalate. A fight is the last thing we want out of this communication.

3. Give An Honest Feedback Where Possible On Their Website

If physical confrontation is not your cup of tea, consider writing in feedback online to express your dissatisfaction. We are usually able to write the most clear and precise account of the situation when we have time to process what went wrong. Instead of handling this confrontation ourselves, the Human Resources team would most likely deal with this person directly, saving you the trouble in the process. Make sure to give an accurate account of the situation and not exaggerate the contents to make the person look extremely in the wrong, although it can be tough to contain our emotions when we are so riled up.

4. Use this Energy To Fuel Your Fire

Sometimes, taking all these energy and intense emotions we feel may fuel our fire to work harder or to prove to others that we are not deserving of their hatred. Be careful though not to take things too far. Remember that ultimately you have the power to choose whether to let this person affect you. If you choose to accept these emotions, use them wisely.

5. Channel This Intense Emotion Into A Craft That Allows You To Release Unwanted Feelings

For those who have musical talents, we may use this negative experience to write a song about it while we are at the heights of our emotions. In those moments the feelings are usually intense, and we all know that emotions can sometimes produce the best works of art. If playing an instrument, writing an article, producing a movie clip, or crushing a sport is something that comes natural to us, we may channel and convert these emotions into masterpieces. Think Adele, Taylor Swift, and all the great songwriters of our generation as an example.

6. Learn To Grow Your Patience

Sometimes not saying anything at all could be the best course of action. Depending on the type of person you are, and the level of zen you have in you, you may not be so easily phased by negativity if you have very high control of your emotions. Through regular meditation and deep breathing, we can let go of these bad vibes that people send our way and just watch it vanish into a cloud of smoke. Regular yoga and meditation practices are good ways to train and grow your patience.

7. Stand Up For Yourself

At the end of the day, you have to choose when and if you want to stand up for yourself if someone has truly wronged you. We can only be so patient and kind to someone before we snap. Never be afraid to speak your truth and defend yourself if you feel that you have been wrongfully judged. Difficult people make our lives unpleasant but it doesn't mean we should allow them to walk all over us without consequences. You have every right to fight for your rights, even if it means giving up something important in the process to defend it.

Chapter 24:

Dealing with Feelings of Failure

Life is full of ups and downs because of which even the strongest person can feel let down. But this doesn't always mean that it's the end. As the famous quote states, "failure is A step closer to success. "Indeed, there are many reasons for feeling hopeless and feeling like you have failed in life, but there is always A way to overcome every type of failure, be it bad grades at school, being let down by friends, or even having problems in relationships. These are some of the many reasons why A person feels like they have failed in life.

The main focus in overcoming this feeling is analyzing the reason for this failure. For example, if A person fails an exam. They should first own this mistake. This is not easy to do, but by doing so, one can become A better person by trying hard next time. There is always A chance of life improvement. Feeling bad is not A bad thing to do as compared to suppressing the feelings. By suppressing the feelings, regrets can build up, which can further lead to bad habits like addiction and self-harm. Staying away from people who live by quotes like "once A failure, always A failure. " These types of people are the reason why others feel like they are no good and have not done enough. If you start believing this, you can never accomplish anything in life.

Developing healthy habits and eating healthy can lead to optimism which in turn leads to accomplishments. Reading motivational books and attending motivational seminars can help you overcome this feeling because they encourage you to try again with your best effort, which is A very good way to achieve success. Even accepting that you have failed is A healthy step because the burden is reduced once you accept your mistakes. Lastly, you need to evaluate what went wrong with the thing that you've failed in. Evaluating your failures gives you an idea about what not to do next time. Failure should not be seen as A threat, and failure is just an opportunity of proving yourself next time. Without failure, there is no chance of betterment.

Failure teaches you many things, and it teaches you that no human being is perfect, and everyone can make A mistake at some point in their lives. People who have not suffered failure are not perfect, they have A very narrow view of the world around them, and they expect perfection in others. They are very difficult to deal with because of their uncompromising nature. A person who has experienced any kind of failure is very accepting when it comes to people who are having A problem with something and are very eager to help them because they can see themselves suffering from failure in the past. This is A very good trait because nowadays, every other person demands perfection.

Failure is never A defeat and should never be seen as A threatening scenario. There is mostly an option to try again, and those who believe in themselves are the ones that come back strong. There is always an option of seeking help from friends or colleagues, so never hesitate to ask. You can always stand taller after falling. The ups and downs in our lives show that we are alive; the single straight line is merely for the dead.

Chapter 25:

7 Ways To Deal with Personal Selfishness

In a society that emphasizes success and personal achievement, placing your needs above those of others feels necessary sometimes. But If you do want to change. Here are a few strategies that you will find helpful in your quest to become less selfish and more selfless

1. Give Other People Your Undivided Attention

To be a good listener, I've learned that you have to let go of your own beliefs—even for just a moment in time. When someone else is talking, you can't be planning your next move or thinking about how your perspective is "better" or more worthwhile. Listening to the people around us promotes closer, less selfish relationships.

2. Put Your Needs On The Last

I've found that sometimes, doing what another person needs rather than what you want ultimately keeps your needs met, too. Do you care what you eat for dinner? Does the laundry have to be done now when a good game is on? Too often, we waste our energy on making a point to just be "right;" when the thing is, there is usually more than one "right" route anyway.

3. Get Off Your High Horse

It always bears repeating: Nobody in this world is more important than anybody else. Everyone is talented, passionate, and kind in their way.

4. Check With Yourself Constantly

I've found that selfishness is like any other bad habit—it can be hard to quit! Try to consistently check in with yourself and reflect on how your attitude has been lately to adjust where needed.

5. Don't Get Caught Up In The Past

If you have acted selfishly in the past, know that it doesn't make you a bad person. People can change, and you can too. To start moving forward in a more positive direction, you have to leave your past in your path.

6. When All Else Fails, Remember This Quote

"If you think only of yourself if you forget the rights and well-being of others, or, worse still, if you exploit others, ultimately you will lose. You will have no friends who will show concern for your well-being. Moreover, if a tragedy befalls you, instead of feeling concerned, others might even secretly rejoice. By contrast, if an individual is compassionate and generous, and has the interests of others in mind, then irrespective of whether that person knows a lot of people, wherever that person moves, he or she will immediately make friends. And when that person faces a tragedy, there will be plenty of people who will come to help." – *Dalai Lama.*

7. Remember That Everyone Is Going Through Something

Any time you're tempted to judge someone or act unkindly, I remember that life is difficult for everyone, and you should give people the benefit of the doubt.

Chapter 26:

Dealing With Stress from All Angles

Stress is something that every human being suffers at some point in their lives. Whether it is A bad day at school or an exam gone wrong, there is no limit to the reasons behind stress. But some people deal with stress which does not only have one reason. In today's day and age, the world has become so fast that people do not have time for themselves. In situations where one gets the feeling of being beaten or lost, one should never give up and should always focus on what is good.

As stated by Dr. Helen Odessky, "I would encourage [you to] try A stress relief activity three times before you give up on it. "She further explains that when A person is undergoing A state of stress, the body resists any relaxation exercise or practice, so trying it out A few times increases the chances of that practice to work. Sometimes, A person's routine can make them stressed, for example, and if somebody wakes up just before the office starts, they would have to rush for the office and is likely to skip breakfast. If this is A trigger for the stress to kick in, stress can be overcome by simply changing the morning routine and giving the body enough time to function properly before the office starts.

The most important thing to notice in A stressful person is that they either breathe too quickly or too slowly because, in A time of stress, breathing is one aspect that often gets ignored. Breathing is the key for the body to function properly, so trying out A simple inhale/exhale exercise in A time of stress can help to overcome it quickly. Another thing one does in A time of stress is that they start to overthink, and the majority of the thought are negative ones. So, according to bizzie gold, who is A personal development and wellness expert, writing down your thoughts in A time of stress is A good way of letting them out. Especially the bad ones. This way, your brain would be at ease, and you can always reflect on these thoughts once the stressful period is over. Physical exercise is another good way to overcome stress as it produces endorphins, which instantly lighten the mood. The repetitive physical movements can help to fend off the bad thoughts and reset the mind, which leads to A stress-free state of mind. Even during A busy day, going for A short workout such as running can help ease the mind. Lastly, A very effective yet ignored way of overcoming stress is cleaning up the space around you. A dirty or messy space can also lead to bad thoughts, so opting for A quick tidy-up is A very good practice for overcoming stress.

Stress is indeed A very harmful feeling which can make the affected person do harmful things like drugs or alcohol, which can further lead to A messed up life. So overcoming stress before it gets A hold of you is always the better option. The exercises explained above may seem very simple but are very effective for people who deal with stress. Being grateful for what you already have is A great way to overcome stress. Find people who make you feel good in your time of need. We only have one life; why not enjoy it fully and not waste it stressing over meaningless stuff.

Chapter 27:

Discomfort Is Temporary

It's easy to get hopeless when things get a little overwhelming. It's easy to give up because you feel you don't have the strength or resources to continue. But where you stop is actually the start you have been looking for since the beginning.

Do you know what you should do when you are broken? You should relish it. You should use it. Because if you know you are broken, congratulations, you have found your limitations.

Now as you know what stopped you last time, you can work towards mending it. You can start to reinforce the breach and you should be able to fill in the cracks in no time.

Life never repeats everything. One day you feel the lowest and the next might bring you the most unpredictable gifts.

The world isn't all sunshine and rainbows. It is a very mean and nasty place to be in. But what can you do now when you are in it? Nothing? Never!

You have to endure the pain, the stress, the discomfort till you are comfortable with the discomfort. It doesn't make any sense, right? But listen to me.

You have a duty towards yourself. You have a duty towards your loved ones. You are expected to rise above all odds and be something no one has ever been before you. I know it might be a little too much to ask for, but, you have to understand your purpose.

Your purpose isn't just to sit on your back and the opportunities and blessings keep coming, knocking at your door, just so you can give up one more time and turn them down.

Things are too easy to reject and neglect but always get hard when you finally step up and go for them. But remember, every breathtaking view is from the top of a hill, but the trek to the top is always tiring. But when you get to the top, you find every cramp worth it.

If you are willing to put yourself through anything, discomfort and temporary small intervals of pain won't affect you in any way. As long as you believe that the experience will bring you to a new level.

If you are interested in the unknown, then you have to break barriers and cross your limits. Because every path that leads to success is full of them. But then and only then you will find yourself in a place where you are unbreakable.

You need to realize that your life is better than most people out there. You need to embrace the pain because all this is temporary. But when you are finally ready to embrace the pain, you are already on your way to a superior being.

Life is all about taking stands because we all get all kinds of blows. But we always need to dig in and keep fighting till we have found the gems or have found our last breath.

The pain and discomfort will subside one day, but if you quit, then you are already on the end of your rope.

Chapter 28:

Develop A Habit of Studying

Life is a series of lessons.
Your education does not end at 16 or 18 or 21,
It has only just begun.
You are a student of life.
You are constantly learning whether you know it or not.

You have a free will of what you learn and which direction you go.
If you develop a habit of studying areas of personal interest,
your life will head in the direction of your interests.
If you study nothing you will be forced to learn and change through tragedy and negative circumstances.

What you concentrate on you become,
so study and concentrate on something that you want.
If you study a subject for just one hour per day, in a year you would of studied 365 hours, making you a national expert.
If you keep it up for 5 years, that's 1825 hours, making you an international expert, all from one hour per day.

If you commit to two hours, you will half that time.
Studying is the yellow brick road to your dream life.

Through concentration and learning you will create that life.
Knowledge opens doors.
Being recognized as an expert increases pay.
Not studying keeps you were you are –
Closed doors and a stagnant income.

If you don't learn anything, how can you expect to be valuable?
If you don't grow, how can you expect to be paid more?
It only becomes too late to learn when you are dead;
until then the world is an open book will billions of pages.

Often what we deem impossible is in fact possible.
Often even your most lofty dreams you haven't even scratched the surface of what you are capable of.

Taylor your study to your goal –
follow the yellow brick road of your design.
Follow the road you have built and walk toward your goals.

If you want to be successful, study success and successful people,
then learn everything you can about your chosen field.
Plan your day with a set time for your study.
I don't care how busy you claim to be,
everybody can spare 1 hour out of 24 to work on themselves.
If not, I hope you're happy where you are,
because that is about as far as you will get without learning more.

Studying is crucial to success whether it's formal
or learning from books and online material at home.
The knowledge you learn will progress you towards your dream life.
If that is not worth an hour or two per day,
then maybe you don't want it enough and that's ok.
Maybe you want something different to what you thought,
or maybe you're happy where you are.

If not, it's on you to do this –
for yourself,
for your family,
and for your partner in life.
It's up to you to create the world you want –
A world that only you know if you deserve.

You must learn the knowledge and build the dream
because the world needs your creation.
Be a keen student of life and apply its lesson
to build your future on a solid and safe foundation.

Chapter 29:

Doing The Thing You Love Most

Today we are going to talk about following your heart and just going for your passion, even if it ends up being a hobby project.

Many of us have passions that we want to pursue. Whether it be a sport, a fitness goal, a career goal, or simply just doing something we know we are good at. Something that electrifies our soul. Something that really doesn't require much persuasion for us to just go do it on a whim.

Many of us dare not pursue this passion because people have told us time and time again that it will not lead to anywhere. Or maybe it is that voice inside your head that is telling you you should just stick to the practical things in life. Whatever the reasons may be, that itch always seem to pester us, calling out to us, even though we have tried our best to put it aside.

We know what our talents are, and the longer we don't put it out there in the world, the longer we keep it bottled up inside of us, the longer the we will regret it. Personally, Music has always been something that has been calling out to me since i was 15. I've always dabbled in and out of it, but never took it seriously. I found myself 14 years later, wondering how much i could've achieved in the music space if i had just leaned in to it just a little.

I decided that I had just about put it off for long enough and decided to pursue music part time. I just knew deep down inside me that if i did not at least try, that i was going to regret it at some point again in the future. It is true that passions come and go. We may jump from passion to passion over the course of our lives, and that is okay. But if that thing has been there calling out to you for years or even decades, maybe you should pay closer attention to it just a little more.

Make your passion a project. Make it a hobby. Pursue it in one form or another. We may never be able to make full careers out of our passions, but we can at least incorporate it into our daily lives like a habit. You may find ourselves happier and more fulfilled should you tap that creative space in you that has always been there.

Sure, life still takes precedence. Feeding the family, earning that income, taking care of that child. But never for one second think that you should sacrifice doing what truly makes you happy for all of that other stuff, no matter how important. Even as a hobby, pursuing it maybe 30mins a day, or even just an hour a week. It is a start, and it is definitely better than nothing.

At the end of the day passions are there to feed our soul. To provide it will some zest and life to our otherwise mundane lives. The next time you hear that voice again, lean in to it. Don't put it off any longer.

Chapter 30:

Don't Fear Judgement

People often seem to get caught up in certain areas of their lives where they have a lot to offer but don't actually have the guts to be transparent about it. Let me make some sense.

We all have this ability to get distracted by things that have very little to do with our actions. But have a lot to do with what others will say about us.

You go through a rough patch in life and then you find the balance. We have things that have been going on in our lives from the beginning, but we still feel doubts about it.

The doubt is natural. But if the doubts are a result of the presence of other people around you, then you have a problem at your hand. This problem is the fear of judgment that everyone imposes on us in their own unique ways.

Humans have a tendency to get out of their ways and try certain things that aren't always normal. They may be normal for some, but for most people out there, it's just another eccentric doing something strange.

So what? What is so bad about being a little different? What is wrong with thinking a little out of the box? Why should your approach be bad if someone doesn't approve of it?

These questions should not make you feel confused. Rather should help you get a much clearer idea of what you want. These questions and their answers can help you find the right motivation. The motivation to do your thing no matter what the others around you say or see.

You are the best judge of your deeds. Because no one else saw your intentions when you started. No one else saw the circumstances that led you to these actions. No other person was in your head looking at and feeling those incidents that carved your present state. But you were always there and always will be.

No one cares what you are up to until you get to the stage of being noticeable. People pass judgments because now you have made it into some sort of limelight. It may be your workplace, your college, or even a party where most people are stoned.

But think about it, what harm can you get with a couple of remarks about your outfit or an achievement?

The words that strike your ears and make you feel incompetent or stupid are just the insecurities of the people around you. The glare of shaming or mockery is only the reflection of the feeling that they don't have what you have.

So be who you are, and say what you want, and do what you feel. Because the people who mind don't matter. But the people who matter would never mind.

Come to terms with yourself and be confident with what you want to do or are currently up to.

No one would understand your reasons and no one is meant to. But they can make a judgment when you are finally on that rostrum. Then you'd have the power to shut anyone at any time.

Chapter 31:

Don't Live Your Life In Regret

Take this for a lesson today; There is no greater pain than that of regret.

Hopelessness is one thing that can crack a soul, but nothing is more hurting than that of lifelong regret. We take up things in our life that we deem helpful for the times to come. But never do we ever take risks, just because we want to have a smooth uncomplicated life.

Life was never meant to be lived as reading off a paper. Neither can you expect it to be a smooth walk on a beach? There are always some pebbles on the way and always some hedges where you need to twist and turn to fit and climb.

We all will eventually o through a period of endless questioning where we judge our every step and every decision whether if it was bad or not good enough!

But why are we indulging in this waste of time when we have so much better things to do right now in this present time slot.

When you are on a long journey, nothing will make sense. When you are on your path to greatness, you will always look back and get drawn back a little every time.

But once you reach the top, you will have a final look back into your past and everything will make sense in a split second.

Life is a roller coaster and we all have baggage. We must have because no one can have lived a long life and have a straight, plain, and colorless script where nothing happened out of the ordinary.

The uncertainty of life is what defines life to its true reality.

We, humans, are a combination of deterministic and non-deterministic behavior where we get triggered on thoughts of shame and failure but rarely do we learn to listen to those failures and try to change our habits.

Things have a course of happening and we always get behind the things that take most of us down the lane. That is where we feel the walk of shame and remember the feeling for the rest of our life.

But why do we feel the urge to remain connected to our shameful past? What needs do we have with feeling shame? Why do we need to remember and regret the things that the world has forgotten a long time ago? Why do we need to keep those memories alive?

A billion incidents are happening every second and we try to keep all our baggage with us till the day we take it with us to our graves.

What we should be doing is to forgive everyone and especially ourselves, to release some positive energy and make some space for the happy times that are to come.

We should let those happy moments erase all our regrets and ease our path for the best future that time could ever earn us. But what you should do ultimately, is to regret what you haven't done yet, rather than what you have done!

Chapter 32:

Enjoying The Journey

Today I want to talk about why enjoying the journey of life is important. And why hurrying to get to the destination might not be all that enjoyable as we think it is.

A lot of us plan our lives around an end goal, whether it be getting to a particular position in our company's ladder, or becoming the best player in a sport, or having the most followers on Instagram or whatever the goal may be... Many of us just can't wait to get there. However, many a times, once we reach our goal, whilst we may feel a sense of satisfaction and accomplishment for a brief moment, we inevitably feel like something is missing again and we search for our next objective and target to hit.

I have come to realize that in life, it is not always so much the end goal, but the journey, trials, struggles, and tribulations that make the journey there worth it. If we only focus on the end goal, we may miss out the amazing sights along the way. We will ultimately miss the point of the journey and why we embarked on it in the first place.

Athletes who achieve one major title never stop at just that one, they look for the next milestone they can achieve, but they enjoy the process, they take it one step at a time and at the end of their careers they can look back with joy that they had left no stone unturned. And that they can live their life without regret.

How many times have you seen celebrities winning the biggest prize in their careers, whether it may be the Grammy's Album of the Year if you are a musician, or the Oscars Best Actor or Best Actress Award? How many of them actually feel like that is the end of the journey? They keep creating and keep making movies and film not because they want that award, even though it is certainly a nice distinction to have, but more so because they enjoy their craft, and they enjoy the art of producing.

If winning that trophy was the end goal, we would see many artists just end their careers there and then after reaching the summit. However, that is not the case. They will try to create something new for as long as people are engaged with their craft, as with the case of Meryl Streep, even at 70+ she is still working her butt off even after she has achieved all the fame and money in the world.

Even for myself, at times i just want to reach the end as quickly as possible. But many times, when i get there, i am never satisfied. I feel empty inside and i feel that I should be doing more. And when i rush to the end, i do feel like I missed many important sights along the way that would have made the journey much more rewarding and enjoyable had I told myself to slow it down just a little.

I believe that for all of us, the journey is much more important than the destination. It is through the journey that we grow as a person, it is through the journey that we evolve and take on new ideas, work ethics, knowledge, and many little nuggets that make the trip worth it at the end. If someone were to hand you a grand slam title without having you earned it, it would be an empty trophy with no meaning and emotions behind it. The trophy would not represent the hours of hard work that you have put in to be deserving of that title.

So, I challenge each and everyone of you today to take a step back in whatever journey you may be on. To analyze in what aspects can you enjoy the moment and to not place so much pressure into getting to the destination asap. Take it one day at a time and see how the journey you are on is actually a meaningful one that you should treasure each day and not let up.

www.ingramcontent.com/pod-product-compliance
Lightning Source LLC
Chambersburg PA
CBHW050030130526
44590CB00042B/2422